사하라아랍민주공화국 헌법

사하라아랍민주공화국 헌법

The Constitution of the
Sahrawi Arab Democratic Republic

도서출판
모래알

우리말 출판에 붙여

사하라아랍민주공화국(서사하라)은 북아프리카 마그레브 서해안에 있는 국가이다. 서사하라는 1976년 2월 27일 독립을 선포했으나 현재까지도 모로코가 영토의 일부를 강점하고 있어 아직 완전히 독립하지 못하고 있다.

서사하라는 1975년부터 모로코와 독립을 위한 투쟁을 벌이고 있다. 이미 41개국이 국가로 승인했으며 유엔 안전보장이사회는 서사하라와 모로코 간의 평화 협상을 촉구하는 결의안을 채택하였으나 모로코는 이를 거부했다. 하지만 서사하라 국민은 독립을 통해 자유롭고 평화로운 사회를 건설하는 소망을 포기하지 않고 오늘도 투쟁한다.

서사하라는 독자적인 정부를 구성하여 체계적인 헌법을 갖고 있기에 모로코의 일방적인 주장과 상관없이 국가로서 그 실제가 분명하다고 할 수 있다.

이 책은 서사하라의 국가 근간인 헌법을 번역한 책이다. 책에서 서사하라가 추구하는 독립의 목표와 정치, 경제, 사회, 문화 등 다양한 분야에 대한 기본적인 원칙을 살펴볼 수 있다. 본 저서를 통해 한국 독자들이 서사하라에 대한 이해를 높일 수 있을 것이다.

서사하라 헌법의 우리말 출판에 도움을 주신 모든 분께 감사드리며 이 책이 양국의 관계 증진에 자그마한 도움이 되길 기대한다.

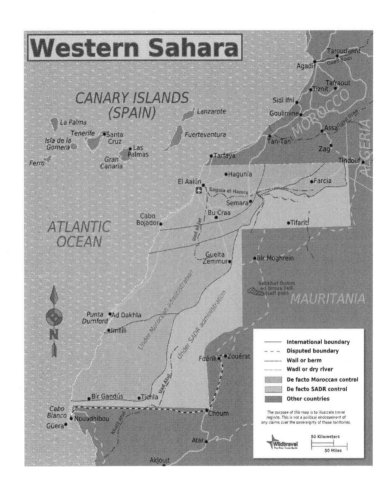

목 차

제 1 부

사하라아랍민주공화국 헌법

한국어본

제14대 폴리사리오 전선 의회 승인,

2015년 12월 16부터 20일

전문

  아랍인이자 아프리카인이며 무슬림인 사하라인은 조국을 식민주의와 점령으로부터 함으로써 우리 민족이 역사 속에서 한 번도 멈추지 않았던 자유와 존엄성을 지키기 위한 저항의 지속을 위해 1973년 폴리사리오전선(Frente Polisario)의 지도하에 민족의 해방을 위한 전쟁을 선포하였고, 우리의 민족적 의지들을 다음과 같이 선언한다.

  사하라아랍민주공화국의 국토 전부에 대한 주권의 회복과 완전한 자주독립을 위한 결의;

세계인권선언(1948년 12월 10일)과 인간과 인민의 권리에 관한 아프리카 헌장(1981년 6월 26일) 그리고 사하라아랍민주공화국이 주체인 모든 국제협약에 명시되어 있는 가치에 대한 존중;

자유와 인간의 존엄성은 법이 자주적이고 사회적 발전을 위한 여건이 그 사회의 가치, 문명, 종교, 국가적 문화와 현대사회의 요구들과 상충하지 않는 경우에만 가능하다는 확신;

자유와 기본권, 사회경제적 권리와 사회를 이루는 가장 기본적인 단위인 가족의 권리를 지키기 위한 민주적 제도를 도입하겠다는 결심;

아프리카와 아랍의 단결, 협력, 조화와 상호존중을 기반으로 한 국제관계의 설립, 그리고 세계평화를 위한 대(大)-마그레브(Maghreb)의 필요성에 대한 인식;

제1장 영토, 국민, 국가

제1절 사기아 엘 하므라와 리오 데 오로

제1조 사기아 엘 하므라와 리오 데 오로(서사하라)는 그 국
제적으로 공인된 영토 내에서 불가분(不可分)한 민주공화국
이며, 이 이후로 그 공식적인 명칭인 사하라 아랍 민주공화국
으로 표기된다.

제2조 사하라아랍민주공화국의 국교와 법의 원천은 이슬람이다.

제3조 사하라아랍민주공화국의 국어는 아랍어이다.

제4조 사하라아랍민주공화국의 수도는 엘 아이운이다.

제5조 국기, 국가(國歌), 국장(國章)은 법률로 정한다.

제2절 국민

제6조 사하라인은 아랍인, 아프리카인이며 무슬림이다.

제7조 가족은 사회의 기반이며, 종교적, 도덕적, 국가적 가치와 역사적 유산을 기반으로 하여 형성되어있다.

제8조 주권은 모든 권력의 원천인 국민에게 있다.

제9조 헌법의 제정 권력은 국민에게 있다.

제10조 국민은 선거를 통해 선택된 대표자들과 헌법을 통해 건립된 국가기관을 통해 주권을 행사할 수 있다.

제11조 국민은 다음과 같은 목표를 지닌 채 주권 행사를 위한 기관을 선택하여야 한다.

1. 그 구성요소를 전부 지닌 국토 전반에 걸친 국가 주권의 회복

2. 국가의 독립

3. 국가적 단결과 국민의 주권에 대한 보호

4. 국민 가치의 보전, 정체성과 국민적 성격의 보호

5. 헌법에 정의된 바와 같이 인간 기본적 자유에 대한 존중의 보장

제12조 국민의 기관들은 국민이 소유한다. 기관 건립의 이유인 헌법적 목표의 달성을 제외한 이유로 악용되어서는 안 된다.

제3절 국가

제13조 국가의 정당성은 국민의 총의(總意)에서 오며 국가는 국민을 위해 봉사한다. 그 금언은 "자유, 민주, 단결"로 한다.

제14조 국가는 영토와 영해 그리고 영공에 대한 주권을 행사한다.

제15조 국토 일부분을 버리거나 할양하는 행위는 금지되어 있다.

제16조 ① 국토는 행정적으로 주(윌라야트), 구(다와이르), 군(발라디아트)으로 나눈다.
② 각 행정구역의 정치, 행정적 권한은 법률로 정한다.

제17조 공공재는 국민에게 그 소유권이 있다. 그 범위에는 광물자원, 에너지 자원, 지하자원, 영토 내의 수자원 및 법률로 정하는 다른 자원들이 속한다.

제18조 국가의 공공재, 기관 및 지역 사회의 정의(定義) 및 관리는 법률에 따른다.

제19조 ① 공직은 축재(蓄財), 사익 추구 및 지역주의, 족벌주의, 부족주의에 기반한 이익 추구의 수단이 되어서는 안 된다.
② 공직을 악용한 행위는 법률이 정하는 바에 따라 처벌한다.

제20조 ① 선거를 통해 선출된 위원회는 국민의 의지 표현 및 공직자 감시를 위한 기본적인 틀로서 작동해야 한다.
② 대통령은 정치 세미나 및 선거 과정을 감시하고 감독하기 위한 국가위원회를 구성하기 위한 대통령령(大統領令)을 선포하여야 한다.

제21조 국가는 공공질서 유지와 인신(人身) 및 재산의 안전에 대한 책임을 지닌다.

제22조 사하라인민해방군(ALPS)은 국가의 군대 및 주권의 보호자이다. 그 의무는 다음과 같다.
1. 독립의 달성
2. 국가적 단결의 보호
3. 국토의 단결 및 통합의 유지와 영토, 영공, 영해의 보호

제23조 사하라인민해방군의 구성과 복무요건은 법률로 정한다.

제24조 사하라아랍민주공화국의 대외정책은 다음과 같아야 한다.
1. 독립과 국토 전체에 대한 국가 주권의 회복과 같은 사하라 민족의 정당한 권리의 보호
2. 사라위 민족의 자결권에 대한 지원
3. 아프리카에 정치적 안정을 가져오고 구성국 간에 협력적인 경제적 관계를 구축하고자 하는 아프리카연합에 대한 지원
4. 국제평화와 안정의 확립 및 정의와 평등에 입각한 세계인의 경제적, 사회적 발전

제2장 헌법상의 권리, 보호 및 의무

제1절 헌법상의 권리와 보호

제25조 모든 사하라 사람은 민족, 인종, 성별, 언어, 종교에
의한 차별 없이 헌법에 보장된 권리와 자유를 누린다.

제26조 모든 사람은 법의 적용에 있어서 평등하다.

제27조 ① 개인의 기본권은 법으로서 보호된다. 그 누구도 법률에 따르지 않고는 누구도 자유의 행사를 거부당하지 않는다.
② 모든 사람은 법률에 따라 그러하지 않다고 판명되기 전까지 무죄로 추정된다.
③ 법정에서 보호받을 권리는 변호인을 선임할 권리를 포함하여 보장된다.
④ 그 누구도 법에 따르지 않고는 체포되거나 구속될 수 없다.
⑤ 법에 규정되지 않은 위법행위 혹은 제재는 있을 수 없다.
⑥ 예방 구금은 72시간 이상 지속될 수 없으며, 법원의 합법적 결정 이외의 방식으로 연장할 수 없다.

제28조 ① 타인의 양심 혹은 명예를 훼손하거나 타인에게 물리적, 정신적 폭력을 가하는 행위는 금지된다.
② 모든 사람의 주거의 불가침은 보장된다.
③ 주거지는 법률에 따라 법원에서 발부된 영장에 의하지 않고는 수색할 수 없다.

제29조 모든 사람은 법원에서 자신의 권리를 보호할 권리를 가진다.

제30조 표현의 자유는 법률에 따라 보호받으며, 그 행사는 법률이 정하는 범위 내에서 행사된다.

제31조 단체 혹은 정당(政黨)을 설립할 권리는 인정되나 독립 이후부터 보장된다.

제32조 국가 주권의 완전한 회복 이전에 폴리사리오전선이 사하라인의 포부 및 독립과 자결권이라는 정당한 권리의 표현, 국가적 통합의 보호와 사하라 국가의 건설을 위한 사하라인의 통합 및 정치적 동원을 위한 정치적 틀로서 작용한다.

제33조 법적 요건에 부합하는 모든 사람은 선거권 및 피선거권을 지닌다.

제34조 모든 사람은 법에 규정된 요건에 부합하는 한, 공직 후보자가 될 권리를 지닌다.

제35조 사유재산권은 법에 따라 보장되며 조직된다.

제36조 ① 교육권은 법에 따라 보장된다.

② 국가는 의무교육과 무상교육을 보장하며 교육에 관한 법에 따라 교육기관을 조직한다.

제37조 ① 모든 사람은 보건 의료와 보호의 권리를 지닌다.

② 국가는 질병과 감염병으로부터 국민을 보호하여야 한다.

제38조 직업의 보유는 모든 사람의 권리이며, 의무이자 명예이다.

제39조 국가는 어머니, 어린이, 장애인, 노인들의 보호를 보장하며, 그 실현을 위해 기관을 설립하고 관련 법률을 홍보한다.

제40조 국가는 모든 사람에게 주거지를 공급할 의무를 지니며, 모든 사람은 법률이 정하는 한도 내에서 거주이전과 주거지선택의 자유를 지닌다.

제41조 국가는 의사(義士)의 부모, 미망인과 그들의 미성년 자식을 포함하여 전쟁에서 부상을 얻은 자, 포로, 해방전쟁의 피해자와 실종자에게 법이 규정하는 물질 및 정신적 권리를 보장한다.

제42조 국가는 여성의 지위를 향상하며 국가건설 및 발전을 위한 그녀들의 정치, 경제, 사회, 문화적 참여를 보장한다.

제43조 국가는 청년층의 지속 가능한 발전 역량 및 그들의 고용을 보장하며, 그들에게 공무에 참여할 권리를 부여한다.

제44조 헌법은 사하라아랍민주공화국 내에 합법적으로 거주하는 국외인들의 종교와 문화적 관습의 향유를 보장한다.

제45조 국가는 합법적으로 거주하는 국외인들의 권리 및 사유재산을 보호한다.

제46조 국가 주권의 완전한 회복 이후, 시장경제와 민간투자는 인정된다. 공공투자 및 개인투자, 해외투자 또한 법으로서 공인되고 규제된다.

제2절 의무

제47조 ① 모든 사람은 헌법과 법률을 존중한다.
② 그 누구도 법에 대한 무지로 사면되지 아니한다.

제48조 ① 모든 사람은 다음과 같은 신성한 의무를 진다.

1. 국가를 보호하고 해방을 위한 투쟁에의 참여

2. 국가적 정체성의 보호 및 국가 이외의 단체에 대한 소속과의 투쟁

② 법률은 반역, 간첩행위, 이적행위 및 국가보안을 훼손하는 범죄를 엄격히 처벌한다.

제49조 국가에 대한 복무는 법률적 요건을 충족하는 모든 사람에 대한 의무이다.

제50조 가족의 보호와 향상, 특히 자식의 교육에 관하여서는 부모의 책임이다. 자식에게도 부모에 대한 존경 및 복종의 의무가 부여된다.

제3장 정부구조

제1절 행정권

제1관 대통령

제51조 폴리사리오전선 사무총장은 대통령직을 겸직한다. 사무총장은 폴리사리오전선 보통회의에서 비밀, 직접 선거를 통해 선출된다.

제52조 대통령은 정책을 지도하고 조정하고, 헌법에 대한 존중 및 법의 집행과 국가기관의 강화를 보장한다.

제53조 ① 대통령은 총리를 임면(任免)한다.

② 대통령은 대통령령(令)으로서 내각을 구성하며, 각 장관의 임무와 권한을 조정한다.

제54조 대통령은 장관회의 의장직을 수행한다.

제55조 대통령은 국회의 승인을 받은 법률에 서명하고 자신의 이름으로서 공포한다.

제56조 대통령은 당선 후 다음과 같은 선서를 한다.

"나는 신 앞에 다음과 같이 엄숙히 선서하니, 나는 5월 20일 혁명의 가치를 보호하고 헌법의 집행을 보호하며 동(同) 헌법을 준수할 것이며, 우리 민족의 자유와 정의를 향한 갈망의 실현 및 모든 사람의 자유와 권리의 보호, 독립의 쟁취, 국가적 보전과 국토의 통합, 사회의 진보와 발전, 고귀한 가치와 전통의 진척을 위하여 나의 모든 힘을 다할 것이다. 신이 나의 증인이시다."

제57조 대통령은 다음과 같은 의무들을 수행한다.

1. 군을 통수할 의무

2. 외교적 방향성을 정하고 그 실현을 위한 정책을 결정할 의무

3. 사면 및 감형을 집행할 의무

4. 공화국에 주재하는 외교관들을 신임할 의무

5. 훈장 및 명예직을 수여할 의무

6. 조약을 체결 및 비준할 의무

제58조 대통령은 다음의 직위를 인선한다.

1. 대통령직과 관련된 직위

2. 외교관과 외교사절의 수장

3. 장관회의

4. 군사기관 및 시설

5. 왈리(도지사)

6. 상급 판사

7. 상급 경비책

제59조 대통령은 국회가 교체되며 공석이 되어 법의 통과가 불가피하거나 국회가 해산되거나 임기가 만료되었을 경우, 긴급한 상황 혹은 헌법이 그 기능을 다하지 못할 때 대통령령을 공포하고 법의 형태로 지령을 내릴 고유한 권한을 지닌다.

제60조 대통령은 그 어떤 경우에도 장관 및 헌법에 규정된 직책에 대한 임면권을 타인에게 위임할 수 없다.

제61조 ① 대통령이 공석인 경우, 국회의장이 대통령직을 겸임한다. 단, 이 기간이 40일을 넘어서는 안 된다.
② 대통령이 공석인 시기가 국회의 해산과 동시에 일어날 경우, 폴리사리오전선의 국가사무국은 위원 중 하나를 임시로 사무총장과 대통령으로 임명할 수 있다. 단, 이 경우에는 헌법 제62조가 적용되어야 한다.
③ 대통령이 공석인 시기가 국회의장이 공석일 때와 겹친다면, 헌법 제83조가 적용된다.

제62조 ① 내각은 대통령의 사망 혹은 탄핵 후 새로운 대통령의 선출까지 해임되거나 재편성되지 아니한다.
② 헌법 제61조에 명시된 기간 동안에는 헌법 제57조와 58조의 권한이 적용되지 아니한다.

제2관 정부

제63조 ① 정부는 국가사무국의 지도를 받으며 행동하는 행정적 기관이며 사무총장과 대통령에게 책임을 진다.
② 정부는 모든 정책, 법 및 규제의 적용에 책임을 진다.

제64조 ① 정부의 인선은 총리가 대통령과의 합의를 통해 선정하고, 대통령이 최종적으로 임명한다.
② 정부의 구성원은 총리에게 책임을 지며, 총리는 대통령과의 합의를 통해 그들을 임면할 수 있다.

제65조 ① 정부는 국가 지도자들의 지도를 통한 국가 정책을 토대로 하여 정책을 구성하여야 한다.
② 총리는 연간의 정책들과 예산을 계획한 후 장관회의에 제출하여야 한다.

제66조 ① 총리는 정부회의 의장직을 수행하며, 그 활동을 감독 및 조직한다.
② 각 부의 장관은 정부 전체에 대한 연대책임을 지고, 자기 부처에 대하여 개별적 책임을 진다.

제67조 정부의 책임, 장관의 조직과 각 부의 책임 및 활동은 대통령령 및 행정지령을 통하여 정해진다.

제68조 정부의 일원은 취임 중에는 명명백백한 죄가 아닌 이상 면책특권을 지니며, 구속되고 수사되지 아니한다. 수사는 총리의 요청과 대통령 재가에 따라 면책특권이 박탈되지 아니하는 한 이루어질 수 없다.

제69조 ① 총리는 정부의 연간 정책 및 예산을 심사를 위해 국회에 제출한다.
② 총리는 국회 심의 과정 중 예산안을 조정할 수 있다.
③ 정부는 국회 재가를 받은 정책에 대해서 국정에 적용한다.

제70조 총리는 타 조항에 따라 부여된 의무 외에도 아래의 의무들을 수행한다.
1. 헌법에 규정된 업무와 헌법 제58조에 있는 정부 구성원에게 직무를 분배하는 의무
2. 행정명령의 발동

제71조 총리는 정부 구성원의 직무를 정지할 수 있고 새로운 장관의 인선을 대통령에게 추천할 수 있다.

제72조 ① 총리는 내각 총사퇴의 재가를 대통령에게 요청할 수 있다.
② 기존의 내각은 헌법에 기반하여 새로운 내각이 완전하게 구성될 때까지 그 직무를 수행한다.

제73조 정부의 구성원은 취임 전 개별적으로 아래와 같이 선서한다.
"나는 신 앞에 다음과 같이 엄숙히 선서하니, 나는 헌법과 법을 존중할 것이며, 나의 명예를 걸고 직무에 성실히 임하고 모든 책무를 완수함으로써 나의 명예와 나의 재량 하의 공공재산을 수호할 것이다. 신이 나의 증인이시다."

제74조 모든 정부 구성원은 법에 따라 재산목록을 대법원장에게 제출하여야 하며, 임기가 만료된 이후에도 동일하게 하여야 한다.

제2절 입법권

제75조 서사하라 국회는 국가의 입법기구이며, 국가의 기관들을 감사할 권한과 법의 초안을 작성하고 통과시킬 독립적인 권한을 지닌다.

제76조 국회는 다음 안건의 통과 여부를 결정한다.

1. 정부의 연간 정책과 예산안

2. 국제조약

제77조 국회는 총 53인으로 구성된다.

제78조 헌법에 따라 한 국회의 만료일로부터 90일 이내에 새로운 국회가 개회되어야 한다.

제79조 국회의원은 보통, 비밀선거를 통하여 선출된다.

제80조 국회의원은 다음과 같은 요건을 충족해야 한다.

1. 서사하라 국적

2. 전과기록의 부재

3. 만 25세 이상

4. 대학 졸업장과 아래 분야에서의 5년 이상의 전문적 경력

가. 합동참모회의의 일원 혹은 군 고위직

나. 외교관 혹은 외교사절의 수장 또는 대표

다. 1회 이상의 국회의원직 수행

라. 큰 규모의 단체에서의 행정 직위 수행

제81조 국회의원의 의무는 국가적 단위의 의무이고 다른 의무와 함께 수행될 수 없다.

제82조 ① 대통령은 국회의 취임 회의에 주재한다.
② 취임 회의는 국가사무국 위원 중 국회의장을 선출하는 데 사용된다.
③ 국회의 선거 과정을 규제하는 법률목록은 회기의 운영 방식과 선거 과정을 규정한다.

제83조 국회의장이 공석이면 그 직은 국회 내 선거에서 차순위 득표자에게 법적으로 이양된다.

제84조 ① 국회의원들은 국민을 대표하고 그들의 원(願)을 대표하며, 자신을 향한 믿음에 충실하여야 한다.
② 의원은 자신의 선거구 내에서 행정부의 행동을 감사할 온전한 권리를 가진다.
③ 의원의 선거를 통한 선출에 유권자들의 과거는 그 어떠한 영향도 끼치지 못한다.

제85조 국회는 의장, 부의장, 위원장과 보고자를 둔 위원회를 지닌다.

제86조 국회는 의장, 부의장과 각 위원회의 위원장을 구성원으로 둔 국(局)을 둔다.

제87조 국회는 사무국장을 그 수장으로 둔 사무국을 둔다. 사무국은 국회 행정과 재무를 국회의장의 감독하에 담당한다.

제88조 ① 국회의 조직과 활동 및 정부와의 관계는 법으로서 정한다.
② 국회는 국가조직에 관련된 법과 헌법에 따라 절차에 관한 규칙을 준비하고 채택한다.
③ 국회의 절차에 관한 규칙은 헌법과 양립해야 한다.

제89조 국회의원은 직무를 수행하는 동안 명명백백한 죄가 아닌 이상 면책특권을 지니며, 구속되지 아니한다. 수사는 법무부 장관의 요청과 대통령 재가에 따라 면책특권이 박탈되지 아니하는 한 이루어질 수 없다.

제90조 ① 국회의원은 자신의 죄로 인하여 명예가 훼손될 가능성이 있는 국회의원에게 해임당할 수 있으며, 동시에 그들에게 책임을 진다.

② 위법행위에 의하지 아니하고 국회의원 직책의 박탈에 대한 요건은 국회의 자체적 규정에 명시되어 있어야 한다.

제91조 ① 국회는 봄과 가을에 매년 두 차례의 본회의를 가진다.

② 각 회의의 기간은 3개월을 넘지 아니한다.

③ 국회는 대통령, 의장, 총리, 혹은 재적인원 3분의 2 이상의 요청에 따라 비상회의를 가질 수 있다. 그 경우는 다음과 같다.

1. 국가적 관심을 요구하는 사건

2. 구성원 중 하나 혹은 이상이 권력의 행사를 위한 요건을 더 이상 충족하지 못할 때

3. 국회의 정상적 직무수행에 대한 중대한 위협

4. 연관된 입법 활동을 해야 하는 사건의 발생

제92조 국회에 설치된 국(局)은 개회로부터 최소 2주 전, 장부의 연간 정책안의 초안을 받는다.

제93조 국회의 각 위원회는 정부의 연간 정책안의 초안에 관한 질문을 준비하고, 청문(聽聞)을 위하여 각 부처의 장관들을 초대할 수 있다.

제94조 ① 국회는 연간 정책안과 예산안에 대해 토의하고 필요에 따라 안의 채택 전에 수정할 수 있다.
② 총리는 국회의 수정을 참고하여 정부의 정책안을 수정할 수 있다.

제95조 만약 세 번의 수정요청 이후에도 재적의원의 3분의 2 이상이 정부의 정책안에 반대한다면, 대통령은 국회를 해산하거나 새로운 내각을 구성할 수 있다.

제96조 ① 각 위원회는 두 회의 사이에도 직무의 수행을 지속하며, 현장 조사와 같은 방법을 통하여 위원회의 담당 범위 내의 정부의 정책 적용을 감독한다.
② 국회의 각 위원회는 세부적 조정과 같은 필요에 따라 정부의 구성원들과 정기적인 회의를 가질 수 있다.

제97조 ① 국회는 지역별로 국(局)을 설치하여 각 지역에서의 정부 정책을 감독할 수 있다.

② 각 지역국의 업무 및 감독의 방식은 정부와 국회의 관계에 관한 법에 따라 결정된다.

제98조 정부는 연간 정책안의 평가보고서를 준비하여 국회의 회의가 있기 최소 1개월 전에 보고서를 제출하여야 한다.

제99조 ① 국회의원은 정부 혹은 그 구성원에게 구술 혹은 기술로서 질문할 수 있다.

② 기술된 질문은 회의로부터 최소 2주 전에 제출해야 한다.

제100조 평가보고서를 국회에 제출한 이후, 정부 혹은 정부의 구성원은 국회의원들로부터의 질문에 답변하여야 한다.

제101조 ① 평가보고서에 대한 토의를 거친 이후, 국회는 정부 관계자를 자신들의 회의에 초대하여 추가적인 설명을 요구할 권리를 가진다.

② 국회는 국가사무국의 위원들을 포함하여 국무에 관한 보고서에 책임이 있는 정부 구성원 모두를 청문을 위해 초대할 권리를 가진다.

제102조 ① 국회는 특수한 관심을 요구하는 안건에 대하여 특별한 조사위원회를 구성할 수 있다.

② 법원의 판결을 기다리는 안건 혹은 주제에 대해서는 조사위원회가 구성될 수 없다.

③ 조사위원회는 그 결과를 국회의장과 공유해야 하며, 국회의장은 제출된 결과를 대통령과 총리에게 공유하여야 한다.

④ 조사위원회는 비공개회의에서 결과를 국회와 공유한다.

제103조 ① 행정부에 대한 감독의 하나로 국회는 내각 혹은 그 구성원을 대상으로 한 불신임안의 투표를 진행할 수 있다.

② 불신임안 요청은 각 의원의 권리이며, 그 토의는 의원 10분의 1 이상이 동의해야 성립된다.

제104조 불신임안은 실정(失政), 의무의 수행에 있어서 중대한 과실, 방임, 공공재산의 낭비, 횡령 및 비효율적 사용 혹은 심각한 비윤리적 행동을 그 근거로 하여 발의될 수 있다.

제105조 국회는 내각에 대한 불신임안은 3분의 2가 동의하고 내각의 특정 구성원에 대한 불신임안에서는 과반수가 동의하였을 때 불신임안을 통과시킬 수 있다.

제106조 ① 국회의장은 대통령과 총리에게 서신을 통하여 내각 혹은 그 구성원에 대한 불신임안이 통과되었다는 사실을 통보해야 한다.

② 내각 구성원에 대한 불신임안의 가장 직접적인 결과는 그 구성원의 해임 및 새로운 인선이다.

제107조 불신임안 통과 이후, 대통령은 15일 이내로 다음과 같은 행동 중 하나를 취해야 한다.

1. 새로운 총리의 선임 및 헌법에 따른 내각의 구성
2. 국회의 해산

제108조 국회가 해산되면 대통령은 40일 이내로 새로운 국회의 구성을 위한 선거를 치러야 한다.

제109조 ① 정부와 국회의원은 법안을 발의할 수 있는 권리를 지닌다.

② 국회 재적의원 5분의 1 이상이 법을 발의한 경우 국회 내에서 토의가 이루어진다.

제110조 국회는 헌법에 따라 정해진 영역 및 아래의 영역에서의 입법행위를 진행한다.

1. 개인의 권리와 의무

2. 가족에 관한 규정

3. 주거에 관한 규정

4. 국적, 시민권 및 지위에 관한 입법

5. 국외인 지위에 관한 규제

6. 사법부의 조직 및 새로운 사법기관의 설립 및 규제

7. 형법과 구속에 관한 규칙

8. 민법, 통상, 사유재산과 공공재산에 관한 규제

9. 국가의 행정구획

10. 세금과 세관에 관한 기관

11. 금융법

12. 교통, 연수, 연구에 관한 규제

13. 공공보건과 주거에 관한 규제

14. 공공서비스에 관한 규제

15. 문화, 역사적 전통에 관한 규제

16. 물질적 권리와 그 조직에 관한 규제

17. 훈장과 명예직의 설립

18. 면책권에 관한 규제

19. 출판, 배포, 정보에 관한 규제

제111조 헌법에 명시된 조직에 관련된 법 이외에도 국회는 이하의 영역에서 조직과 관련된 법에 따라 입법행위를 한다.

1. 공공서비스와 활동의 조직
2. 판사와 최고법무회의에 관한 기본법
3. 국가 보안에 관한 법
4. 선거에 관한 법
5. 변호사에 관한 법
6. 조직에 관한 법은 헌법과의 상성을 보존하기 위해 감독 된다.

제112조 대통령은 법률이 통과되어 제출된 후, 30일 이내에 법을 승인해야 한다.

제113조 ① 대통령은 국회에서 통과된 법률안에 대한 재의를 통과일로부터 30일 내로 요청할 수 있다.
② 대통령이 법률안에 대해 재의를 요청하면 국회 재적의원 3분의 2 이상의 동의로 법안이 통과된다.

제114조 국회에서의 투표는 타인에게 위임할 수 없다.

제115조 대통령은 국회에서 연설할 수 있다.

제116조 국가수반, 정부수반, 고위급 외국대표단은 국회에서 연설할 수 있다.

제3절 사법권

제117조 서사하라의 사법권은 독립적으로 법률에 따라 행사된다.

제118조 판결은 국민을 대리하고 국민의 이름으로 내려진다.

제119조 모든 이는 법적 원칙, 평등과 법에 대한 존중을 그 기반으로 하는 정의(正義)의 적용을 받는다.

제120조 ① 법원은 제1심법원, 제2심법원과 대법원으로 이루어진다.
② 군사법원은 군과 관련된 문제를 관할한다.
③ 그 조직과 기능은 법으로서 정한다.

제121조 법원의 구성, 기능과 권한은 법으로서 정한다.

제122조 대법원은 최고 사법기관이다. 대법원장은 법무부 장관의 추천과 대통령의 임명을 통하여 선임된다.

제123조 검사는 법무부 장관의 추천과 대통령의 임명을 통하여 선출된다.

제124조 모든 정부기관은 때와 장소 및 여타 여건과 무관하게 법원의 판결과 명령을 실행한다.

제125조 ① 법은 소송당사자를 사법기관에 의한 폭력으로부터 보호한다.
② 판사는 임무의 수행과 법의 합치 여부에 대하여 대법원에 책임을 진다.
③ 판사가 헌법에 반하는 행동 혹은 위법행위를 저지르면 대법원에 의하여 처벌된다.

제126조 최고법무회의는 사법부의 최고기관이다. 최고법무회의는 타 기관으로부터 독립되어있으며, 대통령의 임명을 위한 판사를 인선하고, 판사의 물질적, 정신적 권리를 보호하며, 보호의 법제화를 보장한다.

제127조 ① 최고법무회의는 다음과 같이 구성된다.

1. 의장은 대통령

2. 대통령에 의해 임명된 판사 2인

3. 국회에 의해 임명된 판사 2인

4. 판사회의에 의해 선임된 판사 3인

② 각 구성원의 임기는 4년이고 연임할 수 있다.

제128조 ① 국가는 사법부의 독립성을 보호한다.

② 국가는 판사의 의무수행에 악영향을 끼치거나 판결을 치우치게 할 압력과 간섭으로부터 판사를 보호한다.

③ 국가는 판사가 의무를 수행하는 동안, 협박, 망신, 모욕 및 여타 공격으로부터 판사를 보호한다.

④ 국가는 판사가 물질적, 물리적, 정신적으로 가혹한 대우를 받는 경우, 손해 배상에 대한 책임을 진다.

제129조 최고법무회의는 대통령의 사면권과 감형권의 사용에 대한 자문 의견을 제출할 수 있다.

제130조 ① 판사의 권리와 의무 및 법무기관의 구성 및 조직은 법률로 정한다.

② 최고법무회의의 권리, 의무 및 운영은 조직에 관련된 법으로서 정한다.

제131조 변호사는 법률가로서의 직업을 영위하는데 자유롭고 독립적이며, 그 활동은 법으로 조직한다.

제4장 감독 및 자문기구

제1절 헌법위원회

제132조 헌법위원회는 다음과 같은 의무를 지닌 국가기관이다.

1. 법률 및 명령 합헌성의 재확인

2. 국제조약 합헌성의 재확인

3. 선거 합헌성의 재확인

4. 폴리사리오전선 법령 및 헌법의 적용에 관하여 정부기관 사이에서 발발할 수 있는 분쟁의 해소

5. 헌법에 관한 연구의 진행

제133조 ① 헌법위원회는 다음과 같은 위원으로 이루어진다.

1. 대통령에 의해 임명된 위원장

2. 국회에 의해 임명된 위원 2인

3. 최고법무위원회에 의해 임명된 위원 2인

② 헌법위원회 위원은 다음과 같은 요건들을 충족하여야한다.

1. 35세 이상

2. 전과의 부재

3. 법에 대한 전문적 자격과 최소 5년의 법관 혹은 변호사로서의 경력

4. 최소 10년의 정부 부처의 경력

제134조 헌법위원회 위원의 임기는 국회가 교체되는 시기를 포함한다.

제135조 헌법위원회 위원이 임기 중에는 명명백백한 죄가 아닌 이상 면책특권을 지니며, 구속되고 수사되지 아니한다. 수사는 법무부 장관의 요청과 위원장의 재가에 따라 면책특권이 박탈되지 아니하는 한 이루어질 수 없다. 위원장의 경우에는 대통령의 재가로 한다.

제136조 헌법위원회에 대해서는 대통령, 국가평의회 의장 및 총리가 통보한다.

제137조 헌법위원회의 결정은 절대적이며 어떤 형태의 수정 요청도 불가하다.

제138조 헌법위원회의 의무와 운영방식은 절차에 관한 규칙으로 정해진다.

제2절 자문위원회

제139조 자문위원회는 대통령 자문을 위한 조직이다.

제140조 자문위원회의 구성과 운영 방식은 법률에 따라 정한다.

제141조 자문위원회는 대통령령의 규정을 그 운영에 적용한다.

제5장 기타 규정

제1절 종교 및 국가 공휴일

제142조 종교적 휴일은 다음과 같다.

1. 이슬람 달력의 시작

2. 예언자 무함마드의 생일

3. 라마단의 끝

4. 희생제

제143조 국가 공휴일은 다음과 같다.

1. 2월 27일 : 사하라아랍민주공화국 선포일

2. 3월 8일 : 첫 순국자 발생일

3. 3월 10일 : 폴리사리오전선 설립일

4. 3월 20일 : 무장투쟁의 시작일

5. 6월 9일 : 순국자의 날

6. 6월 17일 : 봉기의 날

7. 10월 12일 : 국가통합의 날

제2절 헌법 수정

제144조 ① 국가사무국은 폴리사리오 의회의 국가준비위원회에 수정안을 제출할 수 있으며 국가준비위원회는 국가사무국의 수정안을 의회에 제출하여야 한다.

② 국가 전체의 완전한 주권 회복 이전까지 폴리사리오 의회는 헌법을 개정할 권한을 가진다.

제145조 퇴임하는 전선의 사무총장은 대통령직을 새로운 사무총장의 취임까지 수행한다.

제3장 경과 규정

제146조 경과 기간은 국가 전체의 완전한 주권 회복 이후의 첫 폴리사리오 전선 의회에 의해 결정된다.

제147조 국회는 국가 전체의 완전한 주권 회복 이후의 첫 선거까지 직무를 지속한다.

제 2 부

사하라아랍민주공화국 헌법
영어본

Adopted by the 14th
Congress of the Frente POLISARIO,
16-20 December 2015

Preamble

The Sahrawi people who are an Arab, African and Musl
im people who decided to declare war of liberation in 197
3, under the leadership of the Frente POLISARIO, to libe
rate the homeland from colonialism and subsequently from
occupation, thus continuing the long resistance, which has
never stopped during the history of our people to defend
their freedom and dignity, proclaim:

Their resolve to continue to struggle for the recovery of
the sovereignty of the Sahrawi Arab Democratic Republic
(SADR) over the entire national territory and achievemen
t of total independence;

Their attachment to the principles of justice and democracy as enshrined in the Universal Declaration of Human Rights (of 10 December 1948), in the African Charter on Human and Peoples Rights (of 26 June 1981) and in International Agreements to which the SADR is party;

Their conviction that liberty and human dignity are only possible in a society where law is sovereign and where conditions for social development are created in conformity with the values of the said society, its civilisation, religion and national culture as well as the
demands of the modern world;

Their determination to create democratic institutions that guarantee freedoms and fundamental human rights, economic and social rights and rights of the family, the basic unit of society;

Their awareness of the need to build the Grand Maghre b, to concretise African Unity, Arab Unity and to establish international relations based on cooperation, harmony, mut ual respect and the achievement of peace in the world.

Part 1 Territory, People and the State

Chapter 1: Saguia el Hamra and Río de Oro

Article 1: Saguia el Hamra and Río de Oro (Western Sah ara), within its internationally recognised borders, is a de mocratic republic, indivisible hereinafter known officially as "the Sahrawi Arab Democratic Republic" (SADR).

Article 2: Islam shall be the State religion and a main so urce of law.

Article 3: The official national language shall be Arabic.

Article 4: The capital of the country shall be El Aaiún.

Article 5: The flag, the national anthem and the emblem of the SADR shall be defined by law.

Chapter 2: The People

Article 6: The Sahrawi people are an Arab, African and Muslim people.

Article 7: The family is the foundation of the society; it s hall be based on religious, ethical and national values and on the historical heritage.

Article 8: Sovereignty shall belong to the people who shall be the source of all power.

Article 9: The constituent power shall belong to the people.

Article 10: The people shall exercise their sovereignty through their elected representatives and the constitutional institutions of the State that they may choose to that end.

Article 11: The people shall choose their institutions with the aim of:
- Recovering full national sovereignty over the entire national territory, intact with all its
component parts;
- Attaining national independence;
- Defending national unity and the sovereignty of the people;
- Preserving the values of the people, defending their identity and their national personality;
- Ensuring respect for fundamental human freedoms as defined by the Constitution.

Article 12: The people's institutions shall belong to the people. They shall not be exploited or utilised except for the constitutional objectives for which they have been created.

Chapter 3: The State

Article 13: The State shall derive its legitimacy from the will of the people and shall be at the service of the people. Its motto shall be "Freedom, Democracy, Unity".

Article 14: The State shall exercise sovereignty over its territorial space, territorial waters and air space.

Article 15: It is prohibited to abandon or cede any part of the national territory.

Article 16: The national territory shall be divided administratively into wilayat (Provinces) and dawair (Districts) subdivided into baladiat (Councils).
The political and administrative powers of these divisions shall be defined by law.

Article 17: Public property shall belong to the people. The y comprise the mineral wealth, energy resources, undergr ound wealth, territorial waters and other resources defined by the law.

Article 18: The public property of the State, its various i nstitutions as well as territorial, regional and local commu nities shall be defined and administered in accordance wit h the law.

Article 19: Holding office in the State shall not be a sour ce of personal enrichment nor a means to serve private i nterest or the interests of a group based on regionalism, nepotism or tribalism.
- Such acts shall be criminalised and punishable by the law.

Article 20: The elected Councils shall constitute the frame work within which the people shall express their will and supervise public authorities.

- The President of the Republic shall issue a decree esta blishing a National Committee to oversee the political sem inars and electoral processes associated with them.

Article 21: The State shall be responsible for public order and the security of persons and property.

Article 22: The Sahrawi People's Liberation Army (ALP S) shall be the armed forces of the State and the guaran tor of national sovereignty. Its duties shall include:

- The attainment of national independence;
- The defence of national unity;
- The defence of the unity and integrity of the national t erritory and the protection of theterritorial and air spaces of the State as well as its territorial waters.

Article 23: The organisation of the ALPS and the services within the army shall be defined by law.

Article 24: The foreign policy of the SADR shall be to:
- Defend the legitimate rights of the Sahrawi people to independence and the recovery of their national sovereignty over the entire national territory;
- Support the peoples' right to self-determination;
- Contribute to concretising the unity of the Maghreb where the SADR shall have its own rightful place;
- Support the African Union in its efforts to consolidate political stability in Africa and achieve economic complementarity among its Member States;
- Establish international peace and stability and contribute towards economic and social development of the peoples of the world on the basis of justice and equity

Part 2 Constitutional Rights, Guarantees and Obligations

Chapter 1: Constitutional Rights and Guarantees

Article 25: All Sahrawi citizens shall enjoy the rights and freedoms recognised and guaranteed by the Constitution without any discrimination as to ethnicity, race, colour, gender, language, religion and political or any other opinions.

Article 26: All citizens shall be equal before the law in terms of both protection and sanctions.

Article 27: Individual freedoms shall be guaranteed by the law. No one shall be denied the exercise of his/her freedom except in accordance with the law.

- Every citizen shall be presumed innocent until proven to the contrary by the law;

- The right to defence shall be guaranteed including the choice of a legal representative;

- No one shall be arrested and detained except in accordance with the law;

- There shall be no crime or sanction unless prescribed by the law;

- Preventive detention shall not last more than 72 hours and shall not be extended except on the orders of a competent judicial body and in conformity with the law.

Article 28: It shall be prohibited to violate anyone's sense of morality or honour or to exert any kind of physical or m oral violence against him/her or infringe his/her dignity.

- All citizens shall be guaranteed the inviolability of their domiciles.

- Domiciles shall not be searched expect in accordance wi th the law and with a written warrant issued by the com petent judicial body.

Article 29: All citizens shall have right to defend their rig hts before the competent judicial bodies.

Article 30: Freedom of expression shall be guaranteed an d shall be exercised in conformity with the law.

Article 31: The right to form associations and political par ties is recognised and shall be guaranteed after the attain ment of independence.

Article 32: Until the complete recovery of national soverei gnty, the Frente POLISARIO shall be the political framew ork that shall unite and mobilise politically the Sahrawis t o express their aspirations and legitimate rights to self-de termination and independence and to defend their national unity and complete the building of their independent Sahr awi State.

Article 33: Every citizen who meets all the required legal conditions shall be eligible to vote and be voted for.

Article 34: Every citizen shall have the right to candidatu re for a public office in line with the conditions stipulated by the law.

Article 35: Private property shall be guaranteed and orga nised by the law.

Article 36: The right to education shall be guaranteed.

- The State shall ensure the compulsory and free educati on and organise the educational institutions in line with the educational legislation.

Article 37: All citizens shall have the right to protection a nd healthcare.

- The State shall ensure protection and combat against di seases and epidemics

Article 38: Having employment shall be considered a righ t, an obligation and an honour for all citizens.

Article 39: The State shall ensure protection for mothers, children, disabled persons and the elderly by setting up ins titutions to that end and promulgating the relevant laws.

Article 40: The State shall ensure provision of housing for all citizens who also shall have right to free movement an d the choice of the place of their residence in keeping wit h the laws in place.

Article 41: The State shall guarantee to parents (mothers and fathers), widows of the martyrs, their children who h ave not yet attained the age of majority, those wounded i n the war, prisoners of war, the disappeared and victims of the liberation war, material and moral rights which sha ll be defined by law.

Article 42: The State shall promote women and ensure th eir political, economic, social and cultural participation in t he construction of the society and the development of the country.

Article 43: The State shall ensure sustained capacity buil ding of and the employment of youths and shall empower them to take part in the public affairs of the country.

Article 44: The Constitution guarantees the rights of alien s that reside legally in the SADR territory to practice the ir religions and customs.

Article 45: The State shall guarantee the defence of the r ights and private property of the aliens living legally in th e national territory.

Article 46: After the complete recovery of national soverei gnty, market economy and private initiative shall be recog nised. Public and private investment and foreign investme nt shall also be recognised and regulated by law.

Chapter 2: Obligations

Article 47: All citizens shall respect the Constitution and the laws of the Republic.
- No one shall be excused on account of his/her ignoranc e of the law.

Article 48: All citizens shall be under the sacred obligatio
n to:
- Defend the country and participate in its liberation;
- Defend national unity and fight any semblance of identi
fication other than the identification
with the country;
- The law shall severely punish treason, spying for the en
emy, allegiance to the latter and all crimes committed aga
inst State security.

Article 49: National service shall be an obligation on all citiz
ens who meet the required legal conditions set to that end.

Article 50: The protection and promotion of the family sh
all be an obligation of the parents especially as regards th
e education of their children. It is equally an obligation fo
r children to respect and obey their parents.

Part 3 Organisation of Powers

Chapter 1: Executive Power

Section 1: The President of the Republic

Article 51: The Secretary-General of the Frente POLISA RIO shall be ex officio the President of the Republic. He/ she shall be elected by the General Congress of the Frent e POLISARIO by secret and direct suffrage.

Article 52: The President of the Republic shall guide and coor dinate general policy, ensure respect for the Constitution, the e xecution of the law and the consolidation of State Institutions.

Article 53: The President of the Republic shall appoint th e Prime Minister and shall terminate his/her functions.
- The President of the Republic shall appoint the member s of the Government by a presidential decree that shall i nclude the delimitation of the competences and missions t o be discharged by each minister.

Article 54: The President of the Republic shall preside ov er the Council of Ministers.

Article 55: The President of the Republic shall sign laws that shall be published in his/her name once they have b een approved by the National Council.

Article 56: Upon his/her election, the President of the Re
public shall take the following constitutional oath of office:
"I do solemnly swear by Almighty God that I will defend
the principles of the Revolution of the 20th of May and t
o ensure the execution of the Constitution of the Republic
and to abide by the latter and to be its faithful guardian;
to invest all my energies to concretise the will and aspirat
ions of our people to freedom and justice; to protect the
rights and liberties of all citizens; to ensure the attainmen
t of independence of the country and preserve its integrit
y and territorial unity; to work for the development and
progress of society, and to promote its noble values and t
raditions. God is my witness".

Article 57: The President of the Republic shall perform th
e following duties:

- To be the Commander-in-Chief of the Armed Forces;
- To direct foreign policy and decide on its programmes of action;
- To grant pardon and commute sentences;
- To receive letters of credence of ambassadors accredited
to the Republic;
- To award medals and honorary titles;
- To sign international treaties and conventions.

Article 58: The President of the Republic shall make app
ointments to the following posts:

- Appointments within the Presidency;
- Ambassadors and heads of diplomatic missions;
- Appointments within the Council of Ministers;
- Appointments within Military establishments;
- The Walis (Governors);
- Senior Judicial Officers;
- Senior Security Officers.

Article 59: The President of the Republic shall have the prerogative of issuing decrees and directives in the form o f laws in the interval period between two constituting ses sions of the National Council if there is a pressing need f or legislation, or in the case of the dissolution of the Nati onal Council or expiry of its term, or in the case of an e xtreme case of emergency or when the Constitution is ren dered inoperative.

Article 60: The President of the Republic shall in no circ umstances delegate his/her power to appoint the Prime Minister and other officials in the positions stipulated in t he Constitution.

Article 61: In the case of the vacancy of the post of the President of the Republic, the President of the National Council shall assume the duty of the President of the Re public for a period not longer than forty days.

- In the case that the vacancy of the post of the Presiden t of the Republic takes place in conjunction with the dissol ution of the National Council, the National Secretariat of t he Frente POLISARIO shall convene de jure and appoint a mong its members an interim caretaker that shall discharg e the functions of the Secretary-General and the President of the Republic taking into consideration article 62 below.

- In the case that the vacancy of the post of the Preside nt of the Republic takes place in conjunction with the vac ancy of the post of the President of the National Council, article 83 (paragraph 1) shall be implemented.

Article 62: The Government in office shall not be dismisse
d from its function nor reshuffled in the case of the impe
diment or death of the President of the Republic until th
e assumption of duty by the new President of the Republ
ic elected by the Congress.

- In the interval period defined by Article 61, the provisio
ns stipulated in Article 57 and 58 shall not be applied.

Section 2: The Government

Article 63: The Government is the Executive organ that s
hall operate upon guidance from the National Secretariat
and is responsible to the Secretary-General and the Presi
dent of the Republic.

- The Government shall be responsible for the implementat
ion of all programmes, laws and regulations in all domains.

Article 64: The Prime Minister shall choose the members of the Government in consultation with the President of t he Republic who shall appoint them.

– The members of the Government shall be responsible to the Prime Minister that may terminate their functions in consultation with the President of the Republic.

– The Prime Minister shall not appoint any member in his /her Government without consulting the person concerned.

– Any member of the Government may tender his/her re signation to the Prime Minister.

Article 65: The Government shall prepare its programme of action on the basis of the national programme of actio n and upon guidance of the national leadership.

– The Prime Minister shall prepare the annual programme of his/her Government and the general operating budget, and shall submit them to the Council of Ministers.

Article 66: The Prime Minister shall preside over the Council of Government, supervise its activities and coordinate its work. – The Ministers shall be responsible collectively and in solidarity for the actions of the Government and each Minister shall be individually responsible for his/her Ministry.

Article 67: The responsibilities of the Government, the organisation of Ministries and the responsibilities and functions of the Ministers shall be defined by presidential decrees and other executive directives.

Article 68: The members of the Government shall enjoy immunity during the execution of their duties and shall not be prosecuted and arrested except in the case of flagrant crime or infringement, and shall not be brought to justice until the immunity has been lifted by an explicit request from the Prime Minister and the approval of the President of the Republic.

Article 69: The Prime Minister shall submit the Governm
ent programme and annual operating draft budget to the
National Council for approval.

- The Prime Minister may readjust the programme of his
/her Government in the fight of the deliberations of the
National Council.

- The Government shall implement the programme approv
ed by the National Council.

Article 70: The Prime Minister shall exercise, in addition
to the duties assigned to him/her by other provisions of t
he Constitution, the following duties:

- Assignment of tasks within the Government in conformi
ty with the Constitution and the
provisions stipulated in article 58 thereof;

- Issuance of executive orders;

- Making the appointments delegated to him/her by the
President of the Republic in the appointment decree.

Article 71: The Prime Minister may terminate the functio ns of a member of the Government and propose a new Minister to the President of the Republic for appointment.

Article 72: The Prime Minister may tender the resignatio n of the Government to the President of the Republic.

- The outgoing Government shall continue to exercise its duties until a new Government is appointed pursuant to t he provisions of the Constitution.

Article 73: Members of the Government shall individually take the following oath of office before the President of t he Republic.

"I do solemnly swear by Almighty God to respect the Co nstitution and the laws of the Republic and to execute th em, and I swear upon my honour to work honestly to dis charge my responsibilities and not to damage my reputati on and to preserve the public properties that may be put at my disposal. God is my witness".

Article 74: Each member of the Government shall de jure submit an inventory of his/her private properties before the President of the Supreme Court, and each one of them sha ll do the same upon the termination of his/her functions.

Chapter 2: Legislative Powers

Article 75: The Sahrawi National Council shall be the legi slative body of the country; it shall be vested with the p owers to supervise the State organs and institutions and shall have sovereign authority to prepare draft laws and t o pass them.

- The National Council, within its constitutional prerogatives, shall also exercise the responsibility of financial control over all fixed and movable public assets pertaining to the State.

- In case of misappropriation of public assets, the Preside nt of the National Council shall refer to the Minister of J ustice all cases of misappropriation to be prosecuted in ac cordance with the law.

Article 76: The National Council shall approve:

– The Government's annual programme and general opera ting budget.

– International conventions and treaties.

Article 77: The National Council shall have 53 (fifty thre e) members.

Article 78: A new National Council shall be formed after t he Congress during an interval period of no more than 90 days in conformity with the provisions of the Constitution.

Article 79: Members of the National Council shall be elected by direct and secret suffrage once between two Congresses.

Article 80: Candidates for membership in the National Co
uncil shall fulfil the following requirements:

- To be of Sahrawi nationality;

- Without any criminal record;

- To be of no less than 25 years;

- To have a university degree in addition to five years of
work or a professional experience of no less than five yea
rs in one or more of the following jobs:

- Member of the chiefs of staff of the army or in a senio
r position;

- Member of a regional bureau or in a senior position;

- Central director in a ministry or in a senior position;

- Ambassador, representative or a head of a diplomatic m
ission;

- Member of the National Council for one or more terms;

- Member of the executive board of a mass organisation.

Article 81: The duties of a Council member shall be natio
nal in scope, renewable and shall not be compatible with
other duties.

Article 82: The President of the Republic shall preside ove
r the inaugural constituting session of the National Council.
- The session shall be devoted to the election of the Pres
ident of the National Council among the members of the
National Secretariat.
- The legal list regulating the election process of the Nati
onal Council shall define the modalities for the running of
this session and the methods for carrying out the electora
l process.

Article 83: In case of the definitive vacancy of the post o
f the President of the National Council, he/she shall be r
eplaced de jure by the candidate who obtained the next h
ighest votes among the candidates for the post of the Pre
sident of the Council.
- In case of vacancy of a seat in the National Council, it
shall be filled by the candidate who obtained the next hig
hest votes in his/her electoral district.
- Cases of vacancy of seats shall be defined by the rules
of procedure of the National Council.

Article 84: The member of the National Council shall repre
sent the people and advocate constantly their aspirations an
d shall remain faithful to the confidence placed in him/her.

- The Council Member shall have full right to supervise the a
ctivities of the executive body within his/her electoral district.

- The election of the Council Member shall not be subjec
t to any condition on the part of his/her voters.

Article 85: The National Council shall have a President, a Vic
e-president and Committees with their heads and rapporteurs.

Article 86: The National Council shall have a bureau com
posed of: the President of the Council, the Vice-president
and the heads of committees.

Article 87: The National Council shall have a General Sec
retariat headed by a secretary general that shall be charg
ed with carrying out the administrative and financial busi
ness of the Council under the supervision of the Presiden
t of the Council.

Article 88: An organic law shall define the organisation of the National Council, its activities and functional relations hips with the Government.

- The National Council shall prepare and adopt its rules of procedure in accordance with the Constitution and its organic law.

- The rules of procedures of the National Council shall be compatible with the Constitution.

Article 89: Members of the National Council shall enjoy i mmunity during the execution of their duties and shall no t be arrested except in the case of a flagrant crime or inf ringement and shall not be brought to justice until the im munity has been lifted by an explicit request from the Mi nister of Justice and the approval of the President of the National Council.

Article 90: The member of the National Council shall be responsible to his/her colleagues who may relieve him/her of his/her duties as Council Member if he/she commits a crime that impinges on the honour of his/her office.

- The rules of procure shall stipulate the conditions according to which a Council Member could be expelled from the Natio nal Council without prejudice to any other legal proceedings.

Article 91: The National Council shall meet in two ordina ry sessions: the spring session and the autumn session.

- The duration of each session shall not exceed three months;
- The National Council may meet in an extraordinary session at the request of the President of the Republic or its President or the Prime Minister or two thirds of its members in the case of:
- Extraordinary National events;
- When conditions required for the Government to exercise it s duties are no longer met by it or by one of its members;
- Violations that threaten the normal exercise of the duti es of the National Council;
- Relevant legislative exigencies.

Article 92: The bureau of the National Council shall recei ve from the Government, within a period of at least two weeks before the opening of the session of the Council, th e draft annual programme adopted by the Government.

Article 93: The Committees of the National Council shall pre pare questions on the Government draft annual programme a nd may invite Ministers to obtain the necessary clarifications.

Article 94: The National Council shall discuss the annual pro gramme and draft general operating budget of the Governmen t and propose necessary amendments before their adoption.
- The Prime Minister may adjust the programme of his/her Govern ment in the light of the amendments made by the National Council.

Article 95: In the event that two thirds of the National Council are opposed to the Government's programme afte r having requested its revision for the third time, the Pre sident of the Republic shall either dissolve the National C ouncil or form a new Government.

Article 96: The Committees shall continue to carry out thei r duties between two sessions, and shall supervise the imple mentation of the Government's programme through field visi ts to institutions that fall within their prerogatives with a vi ew to preparing the next session of the National Council.

- The Committees of the National Council may hold perio dic meetings with members of the Government to consider some specific issues.

Article 97: The National Council shall establish regional b ureaus charged with supervision of the programmes of ma nagement and action at regional and local level.

- The organic law regulating the functional relationship be tween the government and the National Council shall dete rmine the modalities of supervision and the work of regio nal bureaus of the National Council.

Article 98: The Government shall prepare an annual assessmen t of its programme that shall be submitted to the National Cou ncil no later than one month before the latter holds its session.

Article 99: Members of the National Council may address oral or written questions to the Government or to one of its members.

- Written questions shall be submitted to Government at least two weeks before the opening of the session.

Article 100: Following the presentation of the assessment of its programme to the National Council, the Government or a member thereof shall respond to the questions raised by the Members of the National Council.

Article 101: Following the debate on the assessment of th e Government's programme, the National Council shall ha ve the right to invite the Government or one of its memb ers for a meeting to provide explanations on one or sever al issues of importance.

- The National Council shall have the right to invite any responsible for a national dossier including members of th e National Secretariat for an interpellation session.

Article 102: The National Council may set up Commission
s of Enquiry to study an issue of particular importance.

- It may not set up a Commission of Enquiry on a matte
r that is before the courts;

- The Commissions of Enquiry shall submit the results of
their work to the President of the National Council who i
n turn shall submit a copy to the Prime Minister and an
other copy to the President of the Republic;

- The Commission of Enquiry shall present the results of
its work to the Council in a closed session.

Article 103: In the exercise of its supervision over the Ex
ecutive, the National Council may vote a motion of censur
e against the Government or against one of its members.

- The request for a motion of censure is the right of eac
h Council Member, and such motion may be discussed onl
y if it has obtained the support of tenth of the Council
members.

Article 104: The decision to censure shall be on the grou nds of maladministration, serious lapses in execution of du ties, negligence, waste of public property, plunder of public property, poor utilisation of public property, failure to mai ntain such property or a serious fault contrary to the ethi cal guidelines of the Government.

Article 105: The National council shall decide on the moti on of censure against the Government by a majority of t wo thirds of its members and by a simple majority for a motion of censure against a member of the Government.

Article 106: The President of the National Council shall s end a letter to the President of the Republic and another one to the Prime Minister to notify them of the decision of the Council to adopt a motion of censure against the Government or one of its members.

- The immediate result of the motion of censure against a member of Government shall be dismissal of the latter and appointment of a new Minister.

Article 107: After the motion of censure against the Gove rnment, the President of the Republic shall react within a period not exceeding 15 (fifteen) days by:

- Appointing a new Prime Minister who shall form a new Gov ernment in accordance with the provisions of the Constitution;
- Or dissolving the National Council.

Article 108: In case of dissolution of the National council, the President of the Republic shall call for early legislativ e elections within a period of no more than 40 (forty) da ys following the dissolution of the Council.

Article 109: The Government and Members of the Nation al Council shall have the right to propose laws.

- The proposed laws shall be subject to discussion if pres ented by fifth of the Council members.

Article 110: The National Council shall legislate in the areas specified by the Constitution and in the following domains:

1. The rights of individuals and their basic obligations;

2. General regulations relating to the family code;

3. The regulations of residence;

4. Basic legislation on nationality, the right of citizenship, civil status;

5. The general regulations on the status of aliens;

6. The regulations on the organisation of the judiciary and the creation of judicial bodies;

7. Rules of sanctions code, penal provisions and the prison regime;

8. The general regulations on the civil code, commercial undertakings and the regime of public and private property;

9. The territorial division of country;

10. Institution of tax and customs code;

11. Finance laws;

12. General regulations on education, training and scientific research;

13. The general regulations on public health and housing;

14. General regulations on the public service;

15. General regulations on the protection of cultural and historical heritage;

16. General regulations on material rights of persons and their organisation;

17. The creation of the State medals and honorary titles;

18. General regulations on immunity (political, legislative and judicial);

19. General regulations on publication, distribution and information.

Article 111: In addition to the areas reserved to the organic la
ws in accordance with the Constitution, the National Council sh
all legislate according to organic laws in the following domains:

- The organisation of public services and their activities;
- The basic law on judges and the Supreme Council of Justice;
- The law on national security;
- The election law;
- The law on lawyers;
- Organic laws shall be subject to supervision to ensure t
heir compatibility with the Constitution.

Article 112: The President of the Republic shall endorse l
aws within 30 (thirty) days starting from the day of sub
mission of such laws.

Article 113: The President of the Republic may request a
second reading of a law, which has been passed by the N
ational Council, within a period of 30 (thirty) days followi
ng the adoption of such law.
- In this case, the law shall be deemed approved upon ado
ption by two thirds of the members of the National Council.

Article 114: Voting in the National Council shall be perso nal and shall not be delegated.

Article 115: The President of the Republic may address t he National Council.

Article 116: Heads of State and Government and importa nt foreign delegations may address the National Council.

Chapter 3: Judicial Powers

Article 117: Judicial powers in the SADR shall be indepe ndent and exercised in accordance with the law.

Article 118: Judgements shall be delivered on behalf of th e people and executed in their name.

Article 119: Everyone shall have access to justice of whic h basis shall be legal principles and equality and respect f or the law.

Article 120: The Courts shall be the Court of First Instance, the Court of Appeal and the Supreme Court.

- Military tribunals shall deal with matters relating to the military establishment.

- Their organisation and functions shall be defined by law.

Article 121: The composition, functions and prerogatives of the Courts shall be defined by law.

Article 122: The Supreme Court shall be the highest organ of the judiciary. Its President shall be a judge appointed by the President of the Republic on the recommendation of the Minister of Justice.

Article 123: The Public Prosecutor of the State shall be appointed by the President of the Republic on the recommendation of the Minister of Justice.

Article 124: All the State organs and institutions shall execute the orders and judgements of the courts at all times, places and in all circumstances.

Article 125: The law shall protect litigants against any br each or abuse from the judicial body.

- The judge shall be responsible to the Supreme Council of Justice as regards the manner in which he/she carries out his/her duties in conformity with the law.
- In the case where the judge acts contrary to the Constit ution or in case of breach of the law, he/she shall be subje ct to disciplinary action by the Supreme Council of Justice.

Article 126: The Supreme Council of Justice shall be the supreme organ of the Judiciary. It shall be independent a nd shall propose judges to the President of the Republic f orappointment, defend the material and moral rights of th e judges and ensure that their protection is legally institu tionalised.

Article 127: The Supreme Council of Justice shall comprise:

- The President of the Republic as President;

- Two judges appointed by the President of the Republic;

- Two judges appointed by the National Council;

- Three judges elected by the general assembly of judges.

- The mandate of each member of the Supreme Council of Justice is 4 (four) years that shall be renewable.

Article 128: The State shall protect the independence of t he judiciary:

- The State shall protect judges against any form of pres sure and interferences that could negatively affect their d uties and the impartiality of their judgement.

- The State shall protect judges against threats, humiliati on, insults and all kinds of aggression as and when they exercise their duties.

- In the case where the judge is subjected to material, p hysical or moral ill-treatment, the State shall be responsib le for paying compensation for the resulting damage.

Article 129: The Supreme Council of Justice shall issue a n advisory opinion on the exercise by the President of th e Republic of the right to grant pardon and commute sen tences.

Article 130: The rights and obligations of judges, and the org anisation and dispensation of justice shall be defined by law.
- The competences, duties and operation of the Supreme Council of Justice shall be defined
by organic law.

Article 131: The legal profession of lawyers shall be free and independent, and shall be organised by a law that de fines its operation.

Part 4 Supervision and Consultative Bodie

Chapter 1: The Constitutional Council

Article 132: The Constitutional Council is a national body charged with:

- Ascertaining the constitutionality of the laws and regulativ e directives;

- Ascertaining the constitutionality of international treaties a nd conventions;

- Ascertaining the legality of elections;

- Settling conflicts that may arise among the State bodies re garding the implementation of the Statute of the Frente PO LISARIO and the Constitution;

- Conducting studies on the Constitution.

Article 133: The Constitutional Council shall comprise:

- The President of the Constitutional Council appointed b y the President of the Republic;

- Two members appointed by the National Council;

- Two members appointed by the Supreme Council of Justice. In accordance with the following conditions:

- To be of Sahrawi nationality.

- To be of no less than 35 years old.

- Without any criminal record.

- To have professional qualifications in law and five continuous years of work in the judicial field or work as a lawyer.

- To have work experience of at least ten years in one o f the national bodies.

Article 134: The mandate of the Constitutional Council shall comprise the interval period between two Congresses.

Article 135: Members of the Constitutional Council shall e njoy immunity during the execution of their duties and sh all not be prosecuted and arrested except in the case of a flagrant crime or infringement and shall not be brought to justice until the immunity has been lifted by an explici t request from the Minister of Justice and the approval o f the President of the Constitutional Council. In the case of the President of the Constitutional Council, the approv al of the President of the Republic shall be required.

Article 136: The Constitutional Council shall be notified b y the President of the Republic, the President of the Nati onal Council and the Prime Minister.

Article 137: The decisions of the Constitutional Council sh all be definitive and shall not be subject to any appeal.

Article 138: The duties and mode of operation of the Const itutional Council shall be defined by its rules of procedure.

Chapter 2: The Consultative Council

Article 139: The Consultative Council shall be a consultati
ve body to the President of the Republic.

Article 140: The composition of the Consultative Council
and the mode of its operation shall be defined by a presi
dential decree.

Article 141: The Consultative Council shall adopt the prov
isions of the presidential decree in its rules of procedure.

Part 5   Other Provisions

Chapter 1: Religious and National Holidays

Article 142: Religious holidays shall include the following:

- The beginning of the Islamic Year (Al-Hijra);
- Birthday of the Prophet Muhammad (Mawlid al-Nabi);
- The end of Ramadan (Eid-Ul-Fitr);
- The festival of sacrifice (Eid-Ul-Adha).

Article 143: National holidays shall include the following:

- 27 February: the Proclamation of the SADR;

- 8 March: First Martyr;

- 10 May: The creation of the Frente POLISARIO;

- 20 May: Commencement of the Armed Struggle;

- 9 June: Martyrs' Day;

- 17 June: Uprising Day;

- 12 October: National Unity Day.

Chapter 2: Amendment to the Constitution

Article 144: The National Secretariat may submit a propo sal of amendment to the National Preparatory Committee for the Congress that in turn shall submit the proposal a mong the documents to be considered by the Congress.

- The Congress shall have the mandate to amend the Co nstitution until the complete recovery of the SADR sovere ignty over its entire national territory.

Article 145: The outgoing Secretary-General of the Front shall continue to discharge the functions of the President of the Republic until the election of a Secretary-General of the Front in the Congress.

Chapter 3: Transitional Provisions

Article 146: The duration of the transitional period shall be determined by the first Congress of the Frente POLIS ARIO to be held after the complete recovery of the SAD R sovereignty over the entire national territory.

Article 147: The National Council shall continue its functions until the election of the first parliament after the complete recovery of the SADR sovereignty over the entire national territory.

사하라아랍민주공화국 헌법

발행 2024년 06월 25일

엮은이 편집부
옮긴이 김준성
발행처 모래알 유한책임회사
출판등록 2019.07.03. (제386-2019-000048호)
발행인 김시연
주소 경기도 부천시 원미구 조마루로 134, 1106동 204호
이메일 MORAEAL20@gmail.com
홈페이지 www.morae-al.kr
ISBN 979-11-981682-9-0 (93360)

값 15,000원